# GOD'S FRONTIERSMEN:

## The Yale Band in Illinois

John Randolph Willis

University Press of America™

**University Press of America, Inc.**™

4710 Auth Place, S.E., Washington, D.C. 20023



Printed in the United States of America

ISBN: 0-8191-0781-6
Library of Congress No.: 79-65011